Grandma's Hands
The Life of Lula Mae

Lula Mae

Grandma's Hands

DEBRA J BRIGHT

Kravitz & Sons
INNOVATORS IN PUBLISHING, MARKETING AND ADVERTISING

Kravitz and Sons LLC
204 E Arlington Blvd. Suite B
Greenville, NC 27858

Published by Kravitz and Sons LLC.

ISBN: 979-8-89639-459-4 (sc)
ISBN: 979-8-89639-458-7 (e)

Library of Congress Control Number: 2026901883

Because of the dynamic nature of the Internet, any web addresses or links contained in this book may have changed since publication and may no longer be valid. The views expressed in this work are solely those of the author and do not necessarily reflect the views of the publisher, and the publisher hereby disclaims any responsibility for them.

TABLE OF CONTENTS

PREFACE

This is my first attempt at writing, so I hope that I do my grandmother justice. I pray that she guides my hand to describe her beauty the best way that I can. I am writing this from my heart, wanting our family (who never had the chance) to know her the way I knew her.

A Beautiful Soul is the best way I can describe Lula Mae. She was my grandmother, and I loved her very much. That is why I'm writing this book, a book written out of love. She was a blessing to me and a blessing to everyone she touched.

For a woman that only had a 2nd grade education, God blessed her with a lot of wisdom. She could do anything and everything, from butchering a pig and using every usable part to wringing the neck of a chicken and cooking it, plus gardening and canning vegetables and fruit. My grandmother could also make her own sewing patterns to make clothes for herself and her family as well as using that skill to also upholster furniture. Lula even taught herself to drive even though she couldn't read or write, I even witnessed her with the hood raised seemingly performing minor repairs! This amazing woman could do farm work and work in tobacco alongside the men. She also possessed the uncanny skill of nursing the sick back to health and that was the reason my father took me to her when I became ill with pneumonia.

God blessed me by putting me with her, a blessing that I am so thankful for. That blessing started when my father brought me to her when I was just 4 months old and continued into adulthood. My first memories were of Lula Mae, she was more of a mother to me than a grandmother.

I will share my memories of this great woman. As I stated, my father brought me to her when I was just 4 months old and Lula was only 44 years old. That visit ended up lasting 4 years. During those 4 years, I not only bonded with my grandmother, but also with my Aunt Geraldine who was 12 years old, and my Aunt Laura who was 13. My uncle Lee was there also and he was 5 years old at that time.

My family are amazed by the things that I remember from those first 4 years. I'm amazed myself, maybe It's because they were such happy memories, memories that I hold dear to my heart, that I will never let go of because they are memories that keeps her close to me. I remember the little white house in Marble Creek, even the layout of the rooms. The wood burning stove in the living room that I fell against and burned my arm. I remember the big barrel at the corner of the house to catch rainwater, which was used to wash our hair. I remember our dogs, rusty and Blacky. rusty was my favorite, she had wavy black hair. I remember walking to the well with my grandmother to fetch water.

Another memory I have is Granny would cook chicken on Sundays. She would wrap it in foil and put it in the back window of the car for us to eat after church. The smell of the chicken would fill the car.

I even remember the end of those 4 years, when they took me home to my father. It was on a Sunday, after church. Just a normal Sunday, we always traveled on Sundays, granddaddy was a preacher who would travel to different churches to preach. But this time they made a detour to Lexington. I had no idea that I was leaving the only home that I ever knew, the only family that I ever knew. I remember daddy coming to Marble Creek to visit me and them telling me he was my father, but he was still a stranger to me. They tried to hand me out the window, I cried and fought for dear life to stay in that car. That was my first heartbreak, being taken away from my grandmother.

Those were my first memories of Lula Mae, the most beautiful woman in the world.

The Beginning

Lula Mae was born December 27th, 1915. She was the only daughter of Grant and Bessie Carter. her parents had five sons and one daughter. her brother's names were Nathaniel, Florin, henry, William Grant, and raymond. She was born at home with the assistance of a midwife. That was how most black children were brought into the world in that time period, at home with the help of midwives. Midwives were a necessity because of racial segregation and living in secluded rural areas, plus hospital births were very expensive and health Insurance was non-existent for a sharecropper.

Lula's childhood was normal, normal for a black child during that time period. She worked the farm during the week and attended church on Sundays. her family attended Clifford Baptist Church in Woodford County. The period that she was raised in was filled with racism and segregation. Kentucky was no different than the rest of the country, maybe a little worse, because it bordered the southern states, where the Jim Crow laws were passed, making it legal to segregate. The arrival of the Great Depression which started in the late 20's made life very hard, so her family survived from her father sharecropping and the food they raised on the farm.

Lula's mother was a housewife who took care of her children and helped work the farm. She was a very fragile woman, who suffered with bouts of depression. her depression led to her committing suicide. It was

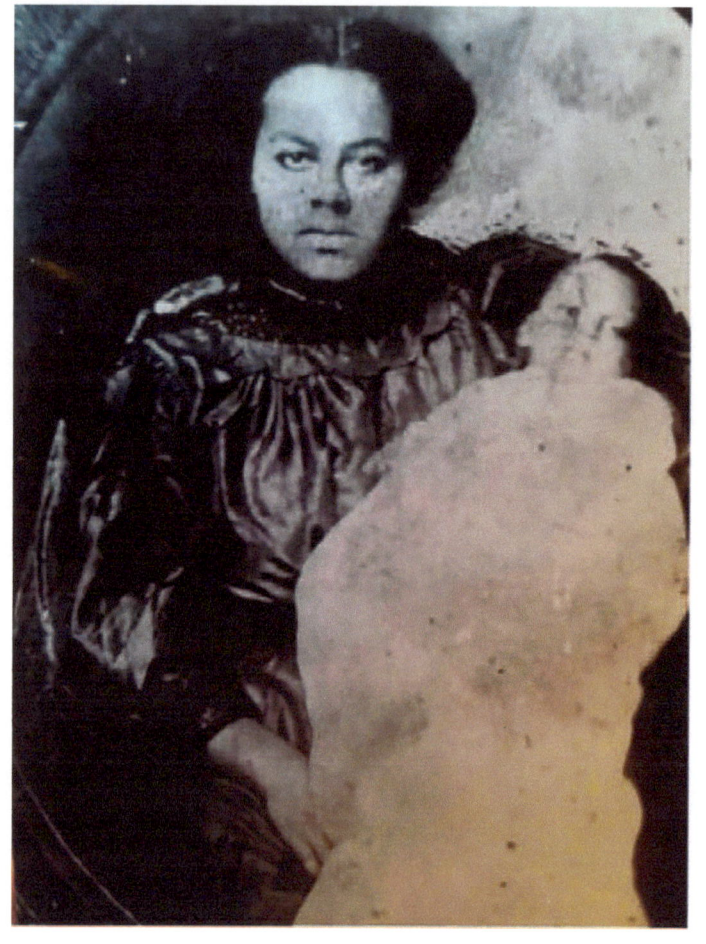

Bessie Carter

said that she made a poisonous tea from the bark of a tree, drank it, and went to bed. She didn't die immediately; it took some time. how much time, is unknown. Lula was only seven years old when her mother died. She watched her fade away, which is a horrible thing for any child to endure. her father did try to help her mother, but she would not allow him in the room. It was said that she laid in bed with a gun by her side and threatened to shoot him if he entered the room.

Bessie's family never cared for Lula's father, so of course, they blamed him. Losing her mother was very hard on her, it was hard on the whole family but harder for Lula Mae, she was a little girl who needed to learn the things only a mother could teach her.

The passing of her mother made her grow up too soon. At seven years old, she became the woman of the house. She had to keep the house clean, cook for her family, and take care of her baby brother, henry. Because of all these responsibilities that she inherited from her mother's death; her father withdrew her from school in the second grade. This wasn't out of the ordinary in those days, a lot of kids were taken out of school to help their family. She was no longer able to be a child and do the things that children did. She had to grow up and grow up fast. her family depended on her.

While taking care of her family, the house, and the farm, she picked up a habit. A habit that she enjoyed and would continue doing for the rest of her life. That habit was smoking. she started smoking at the early age of 8. She did attempt to quit several times throughout her life, but then she would eat more to compensate. Then the weight started piling on, so she went back to smoking. She enjoyed smoking. At the beginning, she rolled her cigarettes, I remember her carrying a little pouch filled with tobacco around her neck. I would watch her take the papers, fill it with tobacco, roll it and then lick it to seal it. I enjoyed watching her roll her cigarettes. That was her only habit, unless you want to consider drinking coffee, a habit. Lula always drank her coffee with cream and sugar. I would ask my grandmother if I could try some but she would tell me no with a smile on her face "because it would make you black"!

A few years later Lula's father remarried. Mrs. Minnie was her name, and she was 18 years old. It made life a lot easier on Lula. her father and Mrs. Minnie had two children together, Mary Sue and Vance (Pete). Now Lula has a total of six brothers and one sister. She still had the responsibility of taking care of the babies. Mrs. Minnie was young and new to being a mother. Lula might have been younger than Minnie but had more experience with taking care of babies, so that responsibility fell on her.

Her father and Mrs. Minnie's marriage lasted just a few years, and their marriage ended in a divorce, not sure the reason. he wasn't alone very long though, he soon married again, and her name was Mrs. Lizzie. he and Mrs. Lizzie had no children together.

As Lula reached her teenage years in the early 30's, she acquired a little more time for herself away from all the kids she helped raise. She still helped her father sharecrop, along with her brothers. Life was very hard in those days, but she did find the time to have a boyfriend. his name was Thomas Parrish. Lula and Thomas had a child together, and they named her Shirley. Shirley was born April 28th, 1932. At 16 years old, Lula's life began as a mother of her own child. She surely had plenty of practice after caring for her brothers and sister for so many years.

MARRIAGE & RAISING HER CHILDREN

Lula Mae and Buford Brown

Three years later Lula met henry Bufford Brown and after a short courtship, they were married. They exchanged their vows in 1935, she was 19 and Bufford was 17. They had their first child a year later, and they named him James. I'm not sure if he was named after Bufford's brother, but he did have a brother named James. James was born June 21st, 1936. Their second child was born the following year, August 30th, 1937. They named him henry, after his father. A year later robert (Bobby) was born, october 16th, 1938. Two years went by and they had another son, my father, Grant, they named him after Lula's father. he was born June 3rd, 1940. Two years went by again and she gave birth to her first daughter with Bufford, and they named her estevior, she was born october 20th, 1942. It was almost exactly a year later that they gave birth to their next child, Vance, who was named after Lula's brother. Vance was born october 24th, 1943.

Marion was born June 7th, 1945, Laura was born April 21st, 1946, Geraldine was born August 14th, 1947, and Sylvester, oops, I mean Lee, he hates to be called Sylvester, was born June 16, 1955. As you can see most of her children were born one or two years apart, except for Lee. She thought she was done after Geraldine, but Lee surprised everyone, he

was a menopause baby. She was 39 years old when she had Lee. Poor woman, she gave birth to a total of eleven children while still helping out on the farm.

The Brown family started on a small farm on Brannon road, between Lexington and Nicholasville. A few years later Bufford moved his family to Marble Creek, just outside of Nicholasville.

The little white house in Marble Creek where Lula and Bufford raised their family. You had to take your shoes off to cross the creek to get to the house. When it rained a lot, the creek would reach the porch, and in the winter the creek would freeze. Geraldine said she remember Aunt Stevey threw her shoes across the creek and missed, so her shoes went floating down the creek. (This little white house still stands as of 2022)

Life was not easy for Lula and her children. Bufford was also a sharecropper, like her father. he raised tobacco for himself and others. She knew life was going to be filled with hard work. They all helped, it was a family function.

Pete Carter

When the family was not working, they were attending church. Lula made sure her children had a strong faith in God, the same as her. They attended Marble Creek Baptist Church, which was just down the road.

All Lula's children started out attending school. They first stared attending school on Brannon road, called Little Zion, then a small one room school in Marble Creek. They later attended school in Nicholasville, which was a school for blacks only. The younger children attended school in Nicholasville after desegregation.

It all ended when Bufford needed the boys to help with sharecropping full time. All the boys were taken out of school to help their father except Lee, who was too young at the time.

Life with Bufford got so bad, that Lula couldn't take it any longer, she had to leave him. She took her remaining children, Vance, estevior, Marion, Laura, Geraldine, and Lee and left her husband. They moved to Grand rapids Michigan with her brother Vance (Pete). They lived there for over a year.

GRANDMOTHER DUTY

Just when she thought she was done raising kids, now she's helping raise grandkids. While Shirley attended beauty school, she was taking care of her boys, russel, Sam, and Wayne, during the week, and Shirley would pick them up on the weekend.

Then Grant brought me, Debra Jean his four-month-old daughter who was sick with pneumonia. he wanted Lula to nurse me back to health, but that nursing lasted four years, that's how long I was there. She became my mother, the only mother I knew. She did have help this time. She had Geraldine, who was twelve and Laura who was thirteen. having a baby in the home for four years, they grew attached and so did I. This was the only home I knew, the only family I knew.

Then the day came that Grant requested his daughter. he had gotten married and was ready for me to come home. It was a hard thing to do, letting go of a baby you took care of for 4 years.

Debra Jean

She found a job as a cook in Miss Kitties restaurant and the kids attended school. Bufford kept begging her to come home, promising that he had changed his ways. he even became a pastor while they were gone. She believed him and decided to return home. her children didn't want to return, they didn't believe he had changed, and they were right. Soon after they returned home he reverted to his old ways, the abuse, and the cheating.

Lula and Bufford's marriage was a rocky one because of his abusive behavior, verbally and physically towards Lula and their children. Bufford was not loyal to Lula, she had to deal with his cheating throughout their marriage. She

Estevior

stayed and endured his abusive behavior and cheating because she loved him. It was also hard for a black woman with kids and no education to make it on her own in those days, so she stayed. She also stayed because of her vows were very important to her. Because of Bufford's abusive behavior, her oldest child Shirley was sent to live with Lula's father and her stepmother, Mrs. Lizzie. This was her way of protecting her daughter. her older sons, James, henry, Bobby, and Grant left home also. They were tired of the abuse and the hard work their father was inflicting on them. Bufford worked all his sons very hard, and they did this with no pay because Bufford kept all of their earnings. Lula's sons were also not happy with the way their father treated their mother, so she knew it was not going to end well. It was time for them to leave to make their own way and get away from their father before something terrible happened. They wanted to hurt their father, and Lula surely did not want her sons in any trouble, especially during that time, when black men were being lynched all over the south. That was just one more thing that black mothers had to worry about. She had seven sons, head strong sons, and didn't want to see any of them in trouble with the law.

A few years later Vance and Marion left home, leaving estevior, Laura, Geraldine, and Lee. Since the older boys were gone, the girls and Lula had to help with the farm and the sharecropping. He would take them out of school to help just like he did with the boys. Lula didn't approve, she wanted her kids to get an education, especially the girls. She didn't want them to end up uneducated like her, she wanted them to have a better life, an easier life than the one she had.

Estevior was the next to leave. She graduated from high school and left for beautician school in Louisville, like her sister Shirley. When she graduated, she refused to return home. She moved in with Shirley till she married George Baker, a boy from a good family in the area. This left Laura, Geraldine, and Lee.

Lula also cared for James boys for a short time, their names were James Allen, who had passed, Vernon, ronnie, and elmer. Their father was in prison, and their mother was not in their life at that time. Their visit only lasted a few weeks.

Later in her life she took care of many more grandchildren. Those grandchildren were so blessed to experience the love of this beautiful woman.

THREE CHILDREN LEFT

Things had not changed between Bufford and Lula but she still stayed. She had three children left and wanted to make sure they graduated and started their own life and hopefully it would be easier than hers. After Laura graduated, she and Geraldine moved out. Geraldine moved to Nicholasville with her sister estevior who was married to George Baker and Laura moved to Lexington. Geraldine completed her last year of high school while living with estevior. They had to leave if they were going to have a chance to graduate, Bufford kept taking them out of school to work on the farm, the same as he did with his sons.

After Geraldine graduated, she, Laura and their cousin Charlene got a place together on ohio street in Lexington Ky. The only child left at home now was Lee. With everyone gone and no one left to help on the farm, Bufford decided to move the remaining family to Lexington.

Laura, Geraldine and Lee

MOVE TO THE CITY

Bufford moved the family to a house on Alabama street. This was a major change for Lula who has always lived in the country. The city noise was the hardest thing for her to get accustomed to, being a woman who had only been familiar with the sounds on a farm, the cows mooing, the chickens cackling, and dogs barking. Now she is going to sleep to the sounds of traffic, neighbors talking, and kids playing because the houses were so close together. There was even an elementary school across the fence in the back yard. Yvonne and I would watch Lee on the playground. Living in the city took some getting used to but the best part of it was, being close to her children. Most of her children were living in Lexington. She could see them more often and they were happy that she lived closer to them.

After moving to Lexington, they also had an addition to the household, Yvonne came to live with them while her father was in prison. She lived with Lula for approximately 3 years.

Moving to Lexington didn't change anything between Bufford and Lula, the abuse and cheating continued. She made up her mind, she could no longer take it. She decided to file for a divorce, all her children, except for Lee was gone. It was time, it was past time for a divorce. She did her best to try and hold her family together but now its time to think about herself and her children supported her decision.

She of course got the house, so after selling it, she had some money to live on. She rented a room in a house across the street from Geraldine and Laura for her and Yvonne. Not sure how long she lived there but she remained till she moved into her own apartment. She moved to Lincoln Terrace on Georgetown Street, where she earned money babysitting.She not only cared for her own grandchildren but had other clients as well. She also made money from ear piercing. Lula did very well for herself. At the age of 55, this was the first time in her life that she had her own place, making her own money, living on her own.

Caring for children was the one thing that she had experience doing. She's been doing it since she was seven years old and she was good at it and loved children. She didn't miss the life of farm work either, it was very hard work and she was now too far up in age to keep doing such hard work. Life was considerably easier now. She could sleep in but continued getting up early in the morning. her body had been programmed to get up with the chickens, she had been doing it all her life. The first thing she did when she woke up was fix herself a cup of coffee, light her cigarette, and watch her soap operas (or stories as she would call them). Soap opera's was one of her pleasures that she discovered after leaving the farm. "As the World Turns", "Days of our Lives", "Guiding Light", "Search for Tomorrow", and "General hospital" were some of her favorites.

FISHBACK

It wasn't long that Lula met Bradley Fishback, a farmer from Stamping Ground Kentucky, which is a small community outside of Georgetown. he wanted to hire her to be his live-in caregiver. Because of her faith, she could not live in the home of a man that she's not married to. he appeared to be a nice old man, a man not in the best health. After a few visits, they decided to marry, but it was more of a business arrangement than a marriage. She was in her mid 50's and he was in his 70's. By this time Lee was not living with her, Vance had Yvonne, and Daddy had me, so she decided to give it a try.

Lula married Fishback and moved to Stamping Ground. This marriage turned out to be more than just care giving. he had a small farm, so she ended up farming and raising tobacco again, along with raising a garden and chickens. Yvonne and I spent a summer with her and would help gather eggs from the hen house which I didn't like because I was afraid of the hens and she would laugh at me because I always returned with no eggs ! We would also pick up rocks out of the tobacco field which I also hated because I was afraid of worms (tobacco worms) unlike my grandmother who wasn't afraid of anything. She did all this while taking care of the house, and him. Fishback didn't honor his part of the arrangement, she was not getting paid. he was a crazy old man, who used her and took advantage of her kindness.I'm not sure how long my grandmother was there but she knew it was time for her to leave, and that's what she did.

GOING WEST

Florin Carter

After the divorce, she wanted to take a trip to Pasadena California to visit her son Vance and her brother Florin whom she hadn't seen for years. This was a much- needed trip after all the stress from dealing with Fishback.

It was beautiful, the weather, and the ocean. She had never seen the ocean before. She had never had the time or opportunity to travel anywhere, except when she left Bufford and went to Grand rapids.

While in California her brother gave her a white dancing poodle, her name was Carol. She was a show dog who had danced on the ed Sullivan show. Whenever a guest would knock at the door she would run to meet them, get up on her hind legs, and dance. She loved that dog. But the next-door neighbor ended up stealing her. She knew it was the neighbor because he kept asking to buy her. She told him no, that she wasn't for sale. one day she let her out and she disappeared. She was living with Marion at the time, and of course he wanted to confront the neighbor, and he did. The neighbor denied it of course. And yes, Marion wanted to beat him up. She told him no, let it go.

MOVING IN WITH MARION

After returning from California, with Lee who had been staying in California with his uncle Florin they moved in with Marion and his son Marion Jr. I moved in also, I was 12 years old. All living in a one-bedroom apartment.I don't know how we did it but we did. There were good memories from that time.I remember she drove a light blue 65 chevy, (what I wouldnt give to have that car now) I can see her sitting on the couch watching her stories on a little black and whit television set with her coffee cup in one hand and her L&M cigarettes in the other while wearing a house dress (which she usually wore).

I wanted to stay up under her all the time.She would always push me off of her, "girl let me breathe" she would say and I would just laugh and lay my head back on her shoulder.I knew her smell, it was comforting and I had been growing accustomed to that familiar smell since I was a baby. one day she locked the screen door and wouldnt let me in, she told me to go make some friends and stop sitting up under her all the time so thats what I did after beating on the door and begging her to let me in didn't work.

Marion Brown

Work As A Caregiver

Henry Carter

Lula moved to Jessamine county with her grandson, Marion jr. to an area known as the "Pocket". It was land owned by the Baker family. She moved there as a live-in caregiver to Mr. and Mrs. Baker. They were the parents of her son-in-law George Baker. She enjoyed her new job and they made her feel like she was part of the family. She attended to Mr. henry Baker till he passed and then remained to continue caring for Mrs. Baker. I'm not sure how long she stayed after that but my granny left because she herself got sick.

After leaving the pocket granny moved to Nicholasville where she stayed with her daughter Stevey for a while. After a short stay with Stevey she then went to back to California to visit with her son Vance, her brother Florin had since passed. During this time Lula found out she had cancer. Because of her illness she moved back to Lexington to stay with her brother henry and sister in law Mae, who was the sister to Bufford. They helped care for her during her recovery, after which she resumed being a caregiver herself which is something she did for the next several years. This was a job she was very good at; it was something she had been doing her entire life. Now it was time for her to stop caring for others and start taking care of herself and enjoy life.

HER OWN PLACE

Granny finally got her own place, she moved to Lexington into a Senior Citizen Apartment. She's done working, done taking care of grandchildren. Now she can rest. She can watch her stories, which is what she called her soap operas, she can drink her coffee, and smoke her cigarettes in peace. She spent the rest of her days going to Church on Sundays and going to Senior Citizens making her crafts. She enjoyed making her crafts and giving them to her family. She had frequent visits from her kids, her grandchildren, and sometimes her great grandchildren. She enjoyed visits from her family, and when they left, they would always leave with a craft she had made.

CALLED HOME

In Loving Memory
of
Lula Mae Fishback

Dec. 27, 1915 - Dec. 27, 2000

Services
1:00, Tuesday, January 2, 2001
St. John Baptist Church
Officiating
Rev., Dr. Jerome Norwood
Interment
Bluegrass Memorial Gardens

Granny wasn't feeling well, found out that her cancer was back. This time she refused treatment. She said she was tired, and didn't want to fight it, she was ready to go. She had a good life, a hard life, but she had her faith, faith in God, whom she accepted at a young age. If it wasn't for her faith, I don't know how she would have endured the heartache of losing her mother at such a young age, the strength of taking care of her brothers when she was a child herself, then raising eleven children while living the backbreaking life of a farmer's wife.

God knew what he was doing, he knew we needed her, her love and her strength. We all have it, we all have it flowing through us, and we will carry it on, through our children, our grandchildren, our great grandchildren, and our future generations. We all have a piece of her inside of us. When you wonder to yourself "where did I get this strength" … now you know, It was LuLA MAe.

On the following pages are some of the descendants of Lula Mae, Starting with the oldest to the youngest and their children, grandchildren, and great-grand- children

SHIRLEY CANADA - *Russell, Samuel Rogers, Wayne*

JAMES BROWN - *Vernon, Ronnie, Elmer, Michelle, Juanita, Rene, Anthony, Carolyn, Willie, Darlene, Renee*

HENRY BROWN - *Tony Edward, Angela, Barry, Lafonda, Lisa*

ROBERT BROWN (BOBBY) - *Gloria, Robert Jr., Melvin, Sondra, Priscilla, Stephanie, Linda, Josh, Jeremiah*

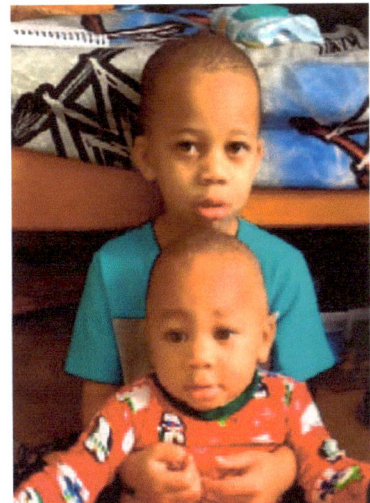

GRANT BROWN *Debra, Grant Jr., Shelia, Sheree, Eric*

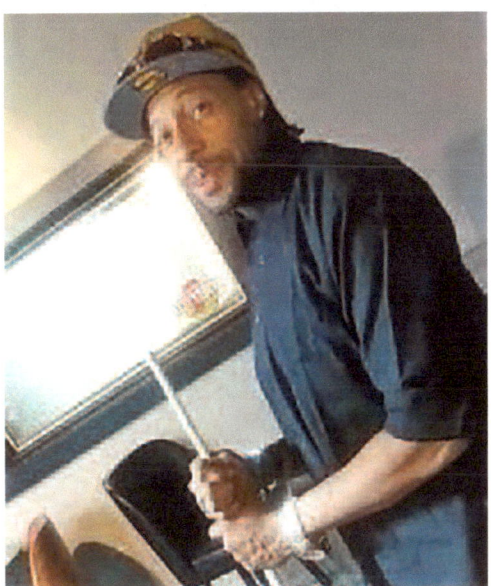

ESTEVIOR BAKER - *Regina, Lana*

VANCE BROWN - *Yvonne, Danyale*

MARION BROWN - *Marion Jr. Kelvin, Orion*

LAURA BAKER BROWN - Maurice, Shana

Family First

GERALDINE MEADS – Gordon, Gregory, and Vanessa

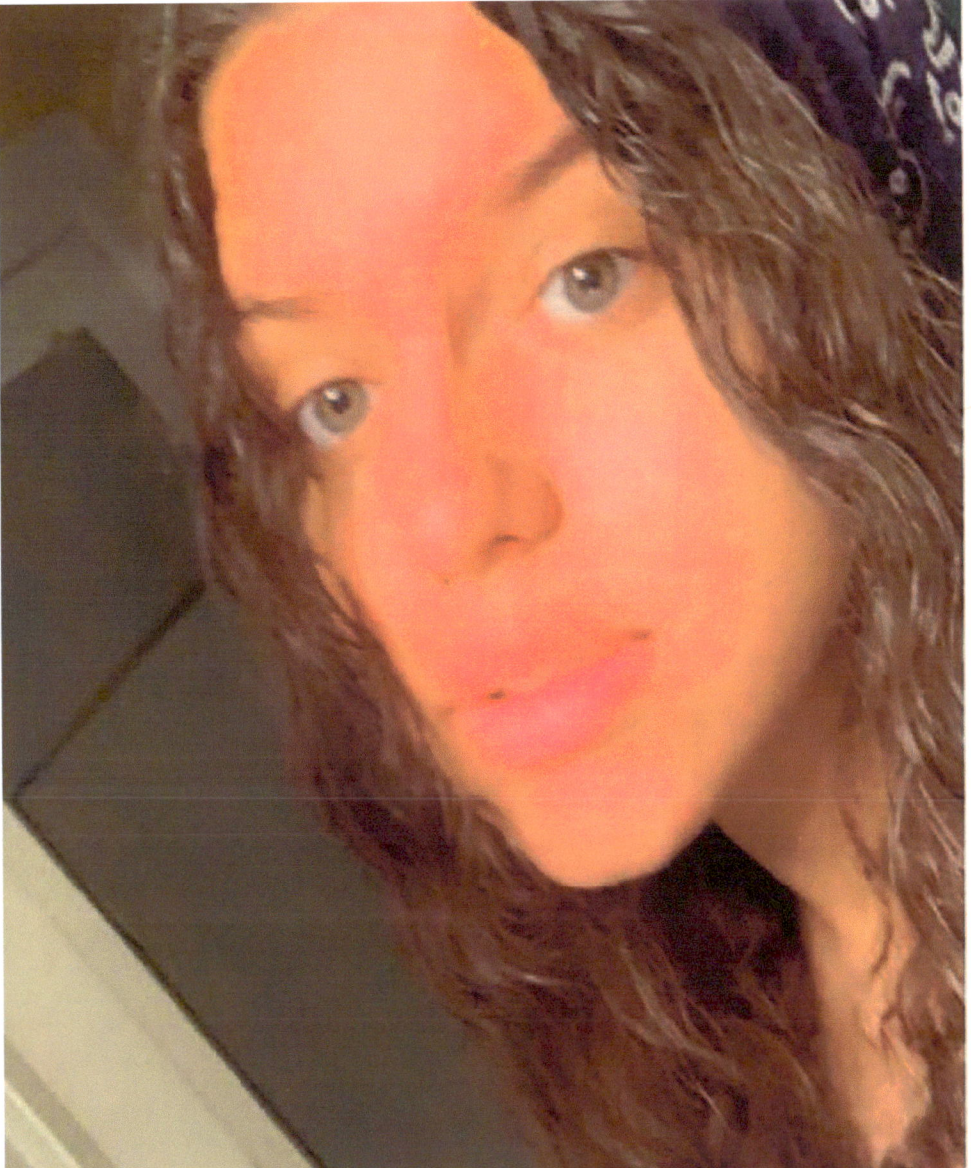

SYLVESTER LEE BROWN - *Mi Chelle and Melissa*

LULA'S FAMILY - Grant Carter, Florin Carter, Laura, Lee, Yvonne, and Lula

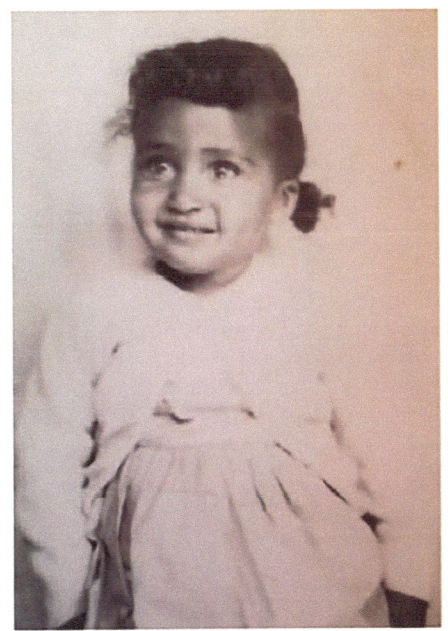

LULA'S FAMILY -
Debra Jean, Gordon Meads,
Maurice, Laura, Geraldine,
Gordon

Lula, Stevey, Shirley,
Geraldine Laura,
Mrs. Mary and Lula

Lula's Sister, Mary Sue and her children Laura, Lee, Yvonne, and Lula

SHIRLEY M. CANADA

1932 - 2007

ROBERT A. BROWN

OCT. 15. 1938
APR. 3. 2012

HE LOVED AND WAS LOVE

LULA M. FISHBACK

REV.
HENRY BUFORD
BROWN
SEPT. 30, 1917
JAN. 15, 1979

MARION L.
BROWN
JUNE 7, 1945.
AUG. 14, 1999

GONE BUT NOT FORGOTTEN